BOOK BENCHERS PUBLICATIONS PRESENTS

Shades of Life

Compiled By

Adline Shami M

Gabrilla Sanchez V

AELAY PUBLICATION

A dream come true for every writers out there. We spot every possible problem for the writers, help in rectifying them and guide them towards the best outcome. We make sure to understand your needs, dreams and expectations, and nourish them with our services and stop not until we fulfill your dreams. The writers have a right and freedom to choose what they want here. They have us to guide them through the hardest path until the end. Believe in us.

Aelay Publication - by a writer for the writers.

BOOK BENCHERS

Book Benchers is the affiliate of Aelay publication. Both the publication is handled by Astro.
Aelay plays the role of publishing solo books. And Book Benchers is epically for publishing anthologies.

Book Benchers have 2 different teams.
1. Tamil

2. English/Hindi

Never mind what our main motive is to help all the budding writers, who are seeking for their dream of publishing their own book to come true.

We are there to help out everyone.
In guiding for starting up with your carrier in compiling until finishing up your full book.

COPYRIGHT

First Edition: October 2021

Design And Executed by

ISBN : 978-93-5533-131-1

Page : 138

<u>ACKNOWLEDGEMENT</u>

God Almighty deserves our gratitude for keeping us all together throughout the anthology.
We would like to express our heartfelt gratitude to the founders of Aelay and Book Benchers Publication, for providing us with such a wonderful opportunity to express our opinions on various aspects of the readers. We are extremely fortunate to be able to work under the auspices of this publishing house.
Furthermore, we are indebted to the co-authors who provided detailed and constructive ideas in their write-ups.

DISCLAIMER

The anthology 'Shades of Life' is a completely original work of a group of aspiring writers. It is assured to be free from plagiarism. In case any plagiarism is found, then the compiler and publication house are not responsible for it.

This is a work of fiction. All the names, characters, business places, events and incidents in this book are either the product of writer's imagination or used in a fictious manner. Any resemblance to actual person, living or dead and actual event is purely coincidence.

<u>FOUNDER</u>

<u>IRUDAGA ASTRO</u>

Irudaga Astro, From Tirunelveli, Founder of
Aelay and BB (Book Benchers)
He had completed his BE.
He has written 3 Tamil poetry book's which hits
the top list on social media!
His main aim is to allow the writers to publish
their words as their book rather than just Posting
them on Insta.

<u>LINK AND POSTER MAKER</u>

CATHERINE ASMI T

Catherine Asmi T, From Tirunelveli
She has completed her M.com
Her passion is Drawing and Designing.

TEAM HEAD

She is a passionate writer from Chennai. Writing makes her pressure go away. She had played the role of co-author for more than 100+ Antho's.

She would like to thank her parents and her Loveable Brother for supporting her rather than stopping her from what she wanted to do! For being the main reason for achieving her dreams. As well as for standing beside her in all the ups and downs.

Whenever she feels like she needs to get out of her stressful timing or feels like she needs peacefulness, she starts to paint, she would never mind sitting in the same place for so many hours when it comes to her painting. She believes that anyone could hurt her, But never her books could!!

Catch her in Insta and FB
Insta: @theinnocentheart
FB: KA. PARINASRI

Book Benchers

COMPILER ©

Adline Shami M

Adline Shami is a blossoming writer. She is a lover of birds and also
an opacarophile. She loves to spend most of her time with the
creations of God. She is a person who believes, a pen is a thing
which gives voice even in silence. She displays her views about the
truth and her love for nature through her poems in an unique way.

LIFE - A LIVELIHOOD

Life is a long road,

Going on and on with lots of snag.

With an unknown cul de sac,

And different shades on it

One to live;

And the other to peg out.

Live life to the fullest;

Learning new things along the way.

Life is complicated:

Gloomy one day and happy the other.

Like a child, laughing and

Shaking it's rattle of death as it runs.

Life is a challenge... Face it,

And when it ends

We find an everlasting peace

Together with the Lord!

CO-COMPILER ©

Gabrilla Sanchez

Gabrilla Sanchez is a free verse writer who has written many poems and quotes on various themes. She has completed her Masters in English Literature and currently doing her M.Phil. Her major works expresses the valley of emotions and life's vision in a different perspective. It also explicates the truth about the existence and human compassion. You can also check out her Instagram page @dreamgirlgaby. According to her, Life is a mixed emotions which lets you to face bitter truths and also the beautiful sides of happiness by surprising you in little moments. Let's explore it and mature together.

MIRACLES!!!

Miracles! The Mighty Miracles,

Literally, the mind asks,

Are you sure about Miracles?

Those Mythical Miracles,

Do they even exist?

But the heartless heart of all centuries,

And the deep inner heart being hypocrite,

Answering, yes! Everyone says so,

The so-called Miracles,

They do exist, you Rookie Brain,

But the heart still wavers,

To believe or not, the Rookie Brain,

Thus, the races began,

Between the Heartless Heart and the Rookie Brain,

And the end always lied in the eyes,

The Key to the realization,

By unlocking the quest for deeper insights,

On the existence of Magic and Miracles.

CO-AUTHORS

1. ASWIN S A
2. JASMINE CHARLOTTE
3. ANUKRAGAH SUNDAR
4. BEULAH MIRACLIN CELEENA S
5. AMY TEPHILLA A
6. SANDRA DAS
7. NEETHU MOL S
8. SHIRLEY GAINNEOS R
9. VIVETHAA
10. BENIJA
11. JAYA SATHYA
12. SATHYA M PILLAI
13. MUTHU MUNIYANDI
14. SUMAIYA
15. WISE MELIENDA HERALD
16. AVNO FEJUST
17. SOPHIA BABY
18. A RAMYA RAJ
19. ADITI MISHRA
20. ROZANA DENIZON
21. S S PRANAV
22. RIYA RICHARD R L
23. D KRISHNA MOHANA SHARMA
24. JEYAMATHI J

25. RESHMA
26. AJAY JAMES
27. SURYA
28. MEHANSHA E
29. ISHIMA KAYALMERIMUS J S
30. ROSHINI M J
31. SHOUMIYA PREETHYPRABAKAR
32. HIMADRI SHEKHAR DUTTA
33. AMBITA C J
34. ZAFFAR IQBAL
35. SILPA SRIKUMAR
36. ANNE NENITA
37. JESSIMA BEGUM
38. J M ROJITH RAJA
39. GREESHMA R P
40. RAMSHA ZAHEEN
41. SMITA
42. ADHITHYA
43. YAMUNA SRUTHI DEV
44. NASRIA M S
45. SATHIYA SEELAN
46. GOLDIN PEARLY J
47. ANALIN SHAJEN
48. TANVI PUNIA
49. NIHHIL S TOMS
50. BENILA

Aswin S.A.

Aswin S.A. is a budding writer. He writes in various themes exploring the true meaning of existence, connecting literature with various aspects of love and life. He writes his poems with extreme passion and all his words are filled with rhyming vividness. There is so much to learn about life from his inspiring lines. He has mastery over vocabulary and syntax, this makes his poems enjoyable. Do read the lines and enjoy for yourselves.

His Insta ID: aswin_s_a

let_me_write_something__

DARKNESS VISIBLE

Darkness is comfortable

When the tidy moon

Pours her Aroma

Like a shower

Darkness is enjoyable

When the crazy moon

Sounds her Love

Like a choir

Darkness is loveable

When the erotic moon

Brings her Desire

Like a fire

JASMINE CHORLOTTE

Jasmine Chorlotte is a budding writer in English. She loves to read modern poetry and haiku. The interest in reading emerges her to write. She focuses on the writings related to nature, love and relationship.

QUEEN OF MY BOSOM: A DAUGHTER'S MOTHER

You are my tranquil Queen

Proving what a daughter should ensue

You are my Shining Gem

Making my inner sense charming

Not the food you feed, the unconditional love you foster

Not the silence you conceive, the amity you made

Not the advice you steer, the moral you master

Not the rest you seek, as a candle you melt

Your smile is luminous day by day

You are my Glowing Star

Countless in sharing your ebb and flow

Intend my thoughts glide consistently

Anukragah Sundar

Anukragah Sundar is a budding writer from Nagercoil. She is well known for her outspoken personality and being studious. She writes devotional poems with deep meanings. She believes in feminism and equality and tries to spread smile wherever she goes.

BEYOND THE SUN

My home is beyond the rising sun,
Where the cloud robed-angels are praising him,
Where the saints are inviting me with them,
To the wonderful heavenly land of Jesus my lord.

I Burry the sorrow in this earth,
Counting the blessings, Thy blessed me with.
I trust in him alone each and every day,
He filled my soul with light and joy today.

Lead me O Lord! Throughout life's darkest hours,
I eagerly await; to reach that place with a flower,
You are the one, and the only king of grace.
When shall I come to thee to see your lovely face?

I know, the cross I gave you is heavy.
I am shattered when I see the cross you carry,
The wealth and the name in this world I burry,
The reward is in heaven so I don't worry.

When he cometh, he calls me by my name,
Waiting for the crown of victory from his hands,
I purchased my pardon from Calvary's cross,
To whom shall I go? But only to thee!

Beulah Miraclin Celeena S.

Beulah is the author of a Christian book, "Ruth - A Detailed Study". She is a well-known blogger, book reviewer and former research analyst. She is a fitness enthusiast, traveler, nature lover and a book nerd, mostly interested in Classics, Thrillers and Historic fiction novels. Beulah spends most of her time reading and reviewing books. She enjoys writing quotes and short poems. Writing helps her to pen down her complex thoughts, in a way to explore her solitary world. She is a homemaker, living in Bangalore with her husband and son.

FLOATING DANDELIONS

Tumbling grey clouds fell upon each other to begin a thunderstorm so scare,

Snapping trees nodded to the fighting wind and let the leaves stir,

There she stood like a drenched flower, pale cheeks mirroring the weather,

With a pour and a drizzle, ruffling breeze ceased the shower,

Drilling a hole through the clouds, a ray of sunbeam caressed her with care,

Turning from golden yellow to feathery white, dandelions flew away with cheer,

Gazing at the floating puffball, her wounds healed to the voice of nature,

Changing from grey to soft orange, the Sun mixed the backdrop for her stare,

Observing the tiny parachutes drifting with the wind to a place so far,

Whirling and flipping the ray florets soared with a cue, abiding by the driving power,

Life is not always grey it muttered, grey is just a shade like every other colour,

Paint your journey with pastels of hue, and make your trip worthy forever!

AMY TEPHILLA A

Amy Tephilla is a person who loves to express her feelings. She believes that message can be conveyed better through writing than speaking. She expresses her thoughts and motivates herself through her writings.

A BIRD WITH THE BROKEN WINGS

I am a bird with the broken wings,

I came out of my mom's egg,

Slowly to the day's light.

I was safe in the nest pot,

Where my mom fed me with her love and care.

Even though I was in the cage,

I was taken care of by the birds inside the cage.

Death followed me,

I fell into the bowl of water,

I couldn't swim out of it,

But an Angel came and saved me.

Now I am out of my nest pot,

Other birds kept an eye on me,

Will I survive or not?

Mom, will you take care of me or not?

With shiver in my body,

I was in the corner of my cage,

I realized I lost one of my wings,

I realized I can't fly anymore,

Other birds looked at me as their prey.

Scared and confused,

What am I going to do?

But here I am!

I didn't breakdown,

I took my steps with strong determination,

I am not scared now,

With my strong will, I am on my own

With my broken wings, here I am!

I will survive stronger and better.

SANDRA DAS

Sandra, a student of English literature and it's her first piece of work. She put a lot of emotions and ideas on her work. And she is a person who is positive at every aspect of life.

PREROGATIVE

The day was a warm morning.

It was pleasant day, with bright ray.

And it was full of blossoms and chirping.

The bird was happy for the day,

So wasn't I.

It was free enough to float,

So wasn't I.

The bird with in me could light;

Hope it know to soar.

But something is holding it badly.

Maybe it is the eyes of star,

Or it can be interiorly.

Every sunset brings

A new dawn's promise.

NEETHU MOL S

Neethu Mol. S, is a beginner of writing poem. She is an English literature student. She started the way of writing herself own and expresses her own views about the poem DEATH.

DEATH

Everything that is alive once eradicate,

It's a part of being;

There is no farewell words to terminate,

The journey's just going;

The soul is never seen, after exit

World becomes a silhouette of memories.

It haste back to Idol, who gave it

Spirit repose peacefully in paradise.

That day everything will be displays,

In the last day of reckoning.

No matter how vigorously death tries,

It can't separate people from loving.

Death ends a life not a relationship

Doomed persons are thy
companionship.

SHIRLEY GAINNEOS R

Dr. Shirley is a dentist and she grew up in Nagercoil, Tamil Nadu. Her interests include singing, reading books, writing, painting and sketching. She has the habit of writing stories and poems ever since she was young. Her inspiration for writing is mainly from reading a lot of books to get an inspiration. And then she applies it, to formulate her own ideas, using her own imagination, to create a poem or a story on whatever thought comes in her mind.

BEAUTY OF NATURE

O Earth! How you are so pure and green,
Filled with flowers with a sparkling gleam,
How beautiful is the land with lush vegetation,
That grows throughout without hesitation.

The air which blows is always purer,
And look! There's a sun which shines brighter!
With the stars and the moon gleaming in the night,
There isn't any worry about day and night light.

The birds fly up in the sky so high,
To hear them chirp makes our heart feel light,
The butterflies flutter at the flowers so bright,
To watch their beauty is a wondrous sight.

How vast is the deep bluish sea,
With lots of fishes swimming so free,
The breeze on the shore do feebly blow,
And the waves of the sea move softly on the shore.

The mountains and valleys make a wondrous view,
Even do the clouds and the forests too.
Just to get a little bit pleasure,
It is best to see and enjoy nature.

VIVETHAA

This is VIVETHAA P, a young budding artist. This is one of my several poems, which were the results of attempt to pen my thoughts and feelings. I'd like to give you a hint to understand my poem better. Me and my brother, were blessed with same zodiac sign (Taurus). As we all know how Tamil people believe in Horoscope, thus made my parents to believe that we should not live together as happily as others, fighting, sharing, and supporting each other. From childhood we were separated, and this made me to pen this poem.

Hope, you'll like my poem. I wish you ALL THE BEST for your success in publishing your anthology. Glad and eager to be in part with you, and I'm soon expecting my poem to be published in your anthology, "Shades of Life."

MY DEAR BROTHER

Born with same blood,

Bloomed under different clouds;

Blessed with same zodiac,

Embellished with unique Psyche;

Forecasting future planned,

Disgusting partition made…

Fleshes are far apart,

Alliance of Spirit knit;

Though each other's' troubling,

However we are siblings;

Thou are my BROTHER,

Love you than all other!!!

BENIJA

She is Benija from Kanyakumari, Tamil Nadu. She is doing M.Sc. Mathematics in Scott Christian College, Nagercoil. She is interested in writing poems in both Tamil and English. She has participated many competitions and got " Thannambikkai Sinthanayalar " award and " Kavi chudar " certificate. She has a YouTube channel for her own poems. Also, she is interested in giving speech and drawings.

LIFE...

Life is like a long-lasting line

By choosing the way of travel through all time

It's all about what we gain

Started with a point of first cry when born

Crossing many troubles using brain

Finding lots of happiness is main

Spreading love is the only wish of mine

Stop worrying about unsavory pain

Start every day with a new dawn

Do what makes you grin

Try to help everyone

Be a Queen to shine

You will be the winner at the end

JAYA SATHYA

This is JAYASATHYA. I am glad to inform you that I am a budding artist, interested in writing quotes, poem and short stories.

MY CHARMING PRINCE

Man of mine,

Make me realize myself

My Prince and nature

Are my ideal companion

He switch my sorrow to Happiness

With potter's magical stick

Others see him as

Dark devil

But he is a person

Who gonna enlight my future

Let me introduce,

My charming prince

Who is none other than?

MY SOLITUDE

SATHYA M PILLAI

The author Mrs. SATHYA M PILLAI MSc, M.Phil. B.Ed is a creative artist and budding writer. She has published and presented number of science articles in national and international seminars & conferences. Recently she has appeared in International Tamil Siragugal event. Right now, she is writing a poetry book in Tamil language. Also, she is one of the managing administrators of Sangathamil Kalaimandram, Kuwait. She has participated in many more small programs, events and writing competitions.

"BE A CHANGER OF A CHANGE"

Intuition of Inner Soul:

The life has many different paths to lead, to progress, to manipulate and to manifest. But many people focus the desire at short period and keep trying to achieve it. Actually, the construction of life has a longer enough distance to create and experience the new ideas and thoughts. The nature of ideas and thoughts emerge from us has a spirit of goodness and uniqueness. Those are the fruits of our conscience, the more ripen fruits will be the more tasty. Bringing taste to our thoughts is a meticulous, harmonious and time lapsing event which allows distinguishing what we can change, what we cannot change and why we change. Pretending it, will be a fallacious and immoral act to the core of life.

Choices:

"Choosing choices are the choice of thoughts and brought ups". Besides the soul thoughts, the social brought up and environmental energies of one self affects more and gives more effects. Human beings are socially evolved. They are easily adaptable to the environmental and social schedules. Apart from the factors of the social inculcations, self-realization and self-understanding gives ability to picture the effects mentally. People who believe self-realization make better choices whereas the mediocre people struggle with handful of opinions, eventually become restlessness. Perhaps, thoughts beyond the current scenario might attract the best choices of path vividly. Sometimes, the nature of the incidents will bring to new heights where people can find the path with clear vision. In addition to that, Allow and accept, are the two aspects of contradictory facts and converting them towards unique desires. This can totally change the notion of the choices.

Patience and time space:

Different choices admire the human being but "The righteous choices are always take time and the courageous attitude never fails to promote it on the particular process of interests". Not a long time, perhaps minimal time of patience opens the entire path of choices smoothly. A person who doesn't have self-control suffers dramatically after pushed into the incident. As a matter of fact, self-control on being patience and giving space are necessary for constant movement on the path. The stereotypical impatient persons may face hardships in their life. The equanimity in every chaos provides the steadiness bring much better solutions. People, who allow such a space of allowance, definitely become more compassionate towards the success of their choices. Such a keen observation of patience one can regulate what we focus and why we change our focus.

Visualization:

The progression of thoughts is the responsible for the happenings in our life. Through visualization of near future results a positive benefits of all happenings even to a good relationships. People who analyses the action- reaction conditions of every incidents will acquire a certain perspectives about it. Such virtual practice may reward the power and zeal to overcome challenges in choosing the best intimidated plans in organized ways. Also the comparison of different selection plans contribute much about where we are, where we want to be, how to get there and mainly it focuses more on why. The virtual image of our progress will have clear objectives in front of us and provides the easy way to check our performances periodically.

Book Benchers

Shades of Life

MUTHU MUNIYANDI

Research Scholar in SASTRA Deemed University

SHE WAS EVERYTHING

She was the lighthouse

When he was directionless in sea of emotions;

She was the Oxygen

 When he was suffocating in despair;

She was the rain

When he was in drought of confidence;

She was the handle

When he was in darkness of fear;

She was the science

When he was in ignorance of ideas;

She was the mother

When he was crying in disbelief;

She was the food

When he was in hungry of hope;

She was the moon

When he was burning like the Sun inside;

She was the smile

When he was about to cry;

She was the treasure

When he was in search of enlightment;

She was the reality

When he was in imagination world.

SUMAIYA

Sumaiya, an Indian poetess (from Tamil Nadu) who wrote under the pen name of SJ. Highly influenced by the regional works, she started to write poems for passion. Currently, she's doing Master Degree in English literature at her region in India.

The Power of Women

Woman can do anything powerful,

Woman is the power of world,

Woman gives birth to child,

Because, Women is the mother of world.

Another name of love is "mother",

A mother's love endures through all,

Women can create a world,

On the other hand,

Women can destroy a world,

Because she plays a role of mother and wife.

God creates men first,

It is "A universal truth", it is from the   "Holy book",

Eventually, Men born from women's womb.

"Women's womb" is the most powerful thing,

Compared to,

All the technology of our world.

Woman is like a glass jar,

Once it cracks,

It surely changes into a powerful weapon.

WISE MELIENDA HERALD

Wise Melienda Herald is a female Indian poet, who was born on 20th August 1994, in Tamil Nādu. She wrote her first poem when she fell in love with her husband, which was not published. This poem 'My second birth' is the first poem to be published. She is the budding writer, who was very much interested in women's equality. She always tries to make others understand the inner agony or pain of a woman. In this poem she writes about her labor pain she underwent during her first delivery. She expresses the sacrifice and tolerance of every woman in this society.

MY SECOND BIRTH

OMG It's 2.00 am already

It's kicking inside readily

Scared in a way to labor

Tears ran away for hour

Whom to call ?, I prayed

Please God I begged

Don't be scared , I told

Be ready…do hold

Now it's 5.00 am, I woke up

I felt kicking like hiccups

Took no break

No doubts it's quake

Striving to breathe easy

Made me messy and uneasy

Dressed up to hospital

Felt like fatal

Entering to the room

Without my groom

Shouted, weaped, mourned

Book Benchers

That horrible day of mine scared

Me, with little anger pleaded

God take me! I surrendered

Entering theatre, to be operated

Bleeded, screaming, a gentleman entered

One push, one shoot

Relaxed my neck to foot

No more pain, I calmed

My eyes were closed

Few more hours to be won.

Felt no touch, I hear someone

It's 3.30 pm, and was like hell

Open your eyes! You are well!

My face went coy out of joy

When I hear 'It's a Boy'.

AVNO FEJUST

J. Avno Fejust is a student of Grade II in Sacred Heart
International School, Pammam, Marthandam. Once his teacher,
asked him to write a Poem on "If I Were a Butterfly" he wrote this
Poem.

Shades of Life

IF I WERE A BUTTERFLY

If I Were a Butterfly

Life begins a New

Cherish forever to Flew

Strive hard to Achieve

Hope for a Renew

Thank God for His Virtue

SOPHIA BABY

C Sophia Baby was born in April 20, 2000 in Trichy. She currently lives in her father's hometown Nagercoil, a town in Kanyakumari, Tamil Nadu. She studied English Literature in Women's Christian College, Nagercoil. The short story "Scammer", is her first published work. The story takes its source from a criminal case in Delhi, which led to the arrest of a big shot who was involved in online scams.

SCAMMER

"In our company, we don't give a shit about our customers," said boss in a muffled voice, as he swallowed the first bite of his chicken puff. However, what he didn't know was as he kept lecturing me, I was lost in my own world of reminiscence-reminiscence of the circumstances that made me end up here.

My mother always knew I was dumb, and I knew that I perfectly took after her.

"Yeh Jeya, how do I open that computer letter writing you showed me that day?", she asked for the hundredth time.

"You mean email Ma? How many times do I have to teach you? Do it yourself," I said annoyed.

Amma had recently developed a new interest for computers. Being a house wife all these years, all she knew was her constant grumbling and nagging. So I taught her to use YouTube on my computer to escape from this daily routine of hers. But as days passed by, Amma became more and more explorative. Learning from YouTube, she troubled me to create a separate email id for her. Her curiosity grew far and wide, as she would go about opening every spam site out there, giving out her email id like it was candy. I knew that one day my computer was going to be loaded with virus, but the pressure of my work did not give me the time to stop her. Again, since I am dumb, I could only land up in a company with a boss who did nothing, but ate chicken puff all day.

"People with a conscience or anything of that sort cannot work here, and you have not pulled off a single successful scam, since you came," said boss, as he slathered ketchup on the puff.

"I wouldn't say that I'm a person of conscience, but you have no idea how smart people are nowadays. It is so hard to scam them," I thought.

After some constant pleading, I managed to return back to my office seat. Our office building holds a dark secret. We are situated on the rear of an innocent sounding travel agency building 'Travo Travels', except that it is just a front for a scamming business call center.

My first call was, from what it sounded, an old English man, maybe at his 60s or 70s.

"Hello, I'm Julia. How can I help you? "I said, searching my computer for the script we usually use to dupe our victims. I was determined to scam him at all cost.

"Hello. Um… I was just trying to watch old movies on my computer and now I've got a computer lock message and there's like a beeping sign that says to ring this phone number," he said, his voice shaking.

"Ok, what were you doing in your computer, when this happened sir?", I asked

"I was only trying to watch movies."

"Do you have an IT guy near you?"

"Uh... No"

"Ok sir, I'll help you then. There must be some service which got broken. This is just a common problem; we need to repair it."

"Yep, I see that."

"Sir, there will be a onetime charge of twelve ninety-five pounds, is that ok?"

"Oh dear, bloody hell! I'll have a heart attack!", he said trembling.

"There must be a lot of virus in your computer. So let me get it done."

The man's voice shook, nearly crying, "I feel sick, Uh… I'm depressed,"

"I now need access to your computer to see what's wrong... Oh don't cry sir, be happy. We're here to help you. You're a good man, don't cry. I can easily fix it once you pay the charge." I said in a loud voice, unable to control my laugh. My fellow scammer colleagues had surrounded me, eager to listen to this fun conversation.

The old fool followed my instructions, downloaded Team Viewer and gave me access to his computer. "There are hundreds of viruses in your computer sir," I said, as I deleted his files to make it look like I was doing something productive in his computer. From the unusual files I saw in his computer, I found out that this wasn't his first time being scammed.

 The old fool did as I said, gave me his identity number and even his credit card details. It was interesting that he didn't realize that he was being scammed. I on the other hand, was delighted, at my first successful scam and at my amazing speaking skills. I felt triumphant like nothing could stop me, as I returned home from my day's work.

When I entered my house, I saw Amma sitting on the floor head on her hand. She was crying her eyes out. The moment she heard my footsteps, she got up and glared at me, teary eyed. "Jeya, we're finished. I got scammed."

A. Ramya Raj

A.Ramya Raj tries to find out the intrinsic bond between life and literature. As a research scholar she tries to depict the life history on Aborigines in Australia. Her writings mainly focus on the reflection of human life.

SHADES OF LIFE

Life is short and sweet with meticulous planning and commend

People are busy with their decorous schedule as some pretend

Cruelty [re]placed the human heart; Shades of Life become colourful part

Children are whites- Heritage of the Lord; yearn for care and rare of their nurture

Teens in red possess energy blood; pillars of the nation immense in fantasy world

Adults in Orange pine for settlement strive harder and vigorous to fulfill their wife

Oldage filled in yellow stretches and sacrifices a lot for their fellow

They awaits for a person to take care of them in mellow

Covid-19 turned topsy turvey the entire human life.

Everyone starts commemorating their overwhelming days

Restarts to yearn for that golden bays

Mask, sanitizer, social distance amplifies presumptuous world

Precautions with covaccine and covishield saves the physic bield

Doctors and nurses frontlline staff became heroes in this field

Humanity knocked the dust off the wield

Bright replaced somber; good over evil;

Virtue against vice; forgive over blame upheavals

Forever it undemands for hedonist to enjoy the survival to petite

Power of mankind blossoms in the shades of life as it is short and

sweet.

ADITI MISHRA

Aditi Mishra was born in 2000 in Meerut, Uttar Pradesh, India. Growing up, She was fascinated with Literature and Psychology and this interest led to some early exposure to reading since she was drawn to stories related to human Psychology, life and suffering. Later, Aditi Mishra, who's now studying Literature at Post Graduate level, developed a passion for ideas. In Thanks' to all those who gave me wings, Aditi explores the issue of how each human suffers no matter what luxurious life he/she is having, how happy people look but they all suffer from inside, They keep the smile on their faces for the sake of others. suffing is an integral part of human life.

THANKS' TO ALL THOSE, WHO GAVE ME WINGS

Thanks' To all those, who gave me wings
But nobody did ever cared that I wanted to swim.
When I read Shakespeare, Virginia Woolf and Oscar Wilde
That moment I realise,
My life is better tragic script write.
I am not a writer but I started to write,
What would I have done, when I saw my dreams flying.
To the people who says
Believe in god for a while, how can I?
I have seen ICU wall's accepting more prayers then temples holy
light,
I have witnessed judiciary providing better justice than Jesus Christ,
I have seen it's not mosque its NGOs that make triple Talaq victim
smile bright.
Sometimes life produce a kind of situation that no scriptwriter can
ever write,
Comical, ambiguous, unpredictable, tragic life is such a multifaceted
sight.
But now I have realised life is not at all about to live for yourself,
But to make others smile Bright.
For all of them I will fly,
Forgetting the fact, once I want to deep dive.

Rozana Denizon

Rozana was an Indian poet. She was born in 21st February 1996 at Kanyakumari, Tamil Nadu. She is a nature lover and poet. This is her first published poem. Her poems are mainly based on love and nature.

ALL MY FANTASY

I was there with my book.
In a garden
 Looked into the blue sky,
Where the misty clouds fly.
The gentle breeze
Play lullaby to my ears.
I fell asleep.
Suddenly, My eyes unbolted.
I catch-sight of,
My prince!!
Leaning over me,
Kissing…. I woke up !!
But he was gone.
Its like magic.
Flutters of thought,
And then I knew.
It was dream,
My fantasy.
Holding the book,
'Sleeping Beauty'.
Made me realize,
I turned into Sleeping Aurora
Waiting to be kissed,
By my Prince Charming
And come back alive into,
The world of love and bliss.

S S PRANAV

S S Pranav is a literary enthusiast, and a student of literature, graduated in English literature from M.S University, Tirunelveli. He himself describes as 'a child' looking astonishingly towards the vast ocean of human experiences, which is "Literature".

THE MOTHER EARTH

The drop of shower from the celestial clouds,

smiling to the Earth, the Mother.

Oh, Mother the Mother of life,

who is the one with the maternal love-

in the court of sun.

The smile in the face of that drop,

is as watchable and loveable as a child-

running towards the Mother's lap, swiftly.

And the supreme Mother with-

an ever-loving embrace, fulfils that await.

That ecstatic little one, lying in the comfort-

of the all tolerant realm of life.

Even though for a while.

Then, subjourns it's way to, leaves and blooms.

With the Mother's legacy.

RIYA RICHARD R L

Riya Richard R. L is a young, burgeoning writer in English. She loves writing from her girlhood. She has a unique style and distinct modus operandi in her writings. She has written more than twenty anthologies. She was born in the most beautiful district Kanyakumari in the most prestigious state Tamil Nadu. She is now an undergraduate in Chemistry, doing her course in Muslim Arts College, Thiruvithancode, in her district. Besides writing, she also loves reading books, drawing, arts and crafts, and learning. She is a lover of Nature. Nature inspires her; she gets most of the ideas, thoughts, and hints from Nature.

I OWE YOU

When I was down and depressed,
You lifted me and cheered me;

When I was shattered and broken,
You recollected and reformed me;

When I was lonely and forsaken,
You comforted me and hugged me;

When I was affected by illness and weak,
You healed me and made me strong;

When I stumbled and fell,
You grabbed me and held me;

When I shed tears of sadness,
You sprinkled drops of happiness;

When I lost and failed in my life
You helped me; I won over strife;

When I was afraid of darkness,
You brought blazing lightness

And effaced the worst worry,
filled my life with best merry;

Without you, I'm nothing
I always Owe you; till the end.

D KRISHNA MOHANA SHARMA

DKM Sharma is currently working as an Associate Professor of English in Vignana Bharathi Institute of Technology, Hyderabad - a reputed autonomous engineering college. He has over 25 years of Teaching experience.

HEARTY LAUGH!

"Respected Principle Sir"
"I am finished my BTech from your esteemed college"
"I am well here and hope you are also in the same well."
Teaching profession has its fair share of amusement. I have always had a hearty laugh coming across such hilariously funny expressions from some of my vernacular background students or even some of my colleagues who are mediocre, if not pathetic, speakers of English. Imagine my shock when I recently came face-to-face with a 'gem of an English Teacher' who overwhelmed and choked me with his 'immense knowledge of English grammar' and his 'felicity and mastery of language and expression.' This outrageously amusing incident took place when the institution where I worked, in the South Indian city of Hyderabad, conducted interviews for faculty positions. And this gentleman in question just walked in to be interviewed like a bolt from the blue!

In fact, this is the second time that I am 'blessed' to have come face-to-face with this gentleman. The first time was when I interacted with (read: interviewed) him for a faculty position to teach English for engineering undergraduates in a college where I worked then. He proved to be quite a handful to me even then. After exchanging some pleasantries, he proceeded with the customary five-minute demo lecture on a topic of his choice. 'Phonetics' turned out to be the topic of his lecture. He started it with a formal definition of phonetics and, as I understood it, wanted to go on with the importance of learning its basics to improve one's quality of pronunciation. He went on to write a sentence on the blackboard which read exactly like this: "Phonetics is the study of the production and articulation of speech, sounds". He said it aloud as he wrote the sentence and repeated it rather slowly and loudly when I, rather embarrassed, requested him to check it again. He sounded quite confident with the comma separating the words speech and sounds when I asked him whether it was intentional or merely an inadvertent error. I, somewhat sheepishly this time, asked him what if the comma was removed not quite understanding what purpose it was serving in that sentence. He emphatically made it clear that the comma was essential as the sentence was an 'accurate' definition of Phonetics and that definitions are generally taken verbatim (he did not use this word, of course). I was baffled when I heard him even mentioning that whether or not comma was there it would not make any difference to the meaning of the sentence! He blah blahed for some more time before we signalled to him to stop. My other colleagues sitting with me did not feel like asking any more questions as they might have been convinced of his 'felicity and proficiency' of the language. We took leave of him saying we would get back to him after a few days. That we never contacted him subsequently goes without saying.

I did not hear much of him until this eventful day when he appeared once again to be interviewed. Sitting along with me on the interview panel was our Head of the Department, an accomplished mathematics professor and author of a few textbooks. The interaction started with his self-introduction during which he mentioned that he was presently working with a reputed group of educational institutions and that he was also the Head of his Department. He also conducted FDPs (Faculty Development Programmes) and Soft Skills Workshops for the students and the staff of his entire group of institutions, he added. He sounded quite confident when he asked us to give him a topic for a demo lecture, politely brushing aside our suggestion that he could go for a topic of his choice. I suggested that he could choose some simple but tricky grammar item. 'Voice' was agreed upon. He began by giving the usual definition and the age-old examples. Then he talked about how some vernacular speakers wrongly use passive forms when active sentences were just enough and gave a sentence as an example: 'I am finished the work' in place of 'I finished the work'. 'Fine', we thought as our HoD looked at me and nodded agreeably. Stretching the topic a little further, I asked him what a sentence like 'I am finished' meant. To our amazement, he said that such a sentence did not exist and it was wrong to use it. He persisted with that even as I told him that I had heard people using that several times. 'How about, "I am done?" I asked then. Again the same answer – that it was grammatically wrong! I decided to quickly wind up the proceedings and asked him something elementary. I asked whether he could convert some active sentences into passive. This I did more to allow him to get back into his comfort zone by falling back on something familiar; or so I thought. After giving him some basic active sentences like, 'Rama killed Ravana' and 'Raju plays cricket', I got a bit naughty and deliberately asked him to convert 'I laughed heartily' expecting the obvious and familiar response that I usually got from my students that it could not be converted into passive since there was no object in the sentence. I was totally caught unawares when my learned friend actually wrote this sentence on the board: 'I WAS LAUGHED HEARTILY'.

Though he took my phone number after the interviews, I was not expecting a phone call that soon so I was a bit confused when I received one from this man the same evening. I was literally flabbergasted when he casually started inquiring about his prospects and asking general questions about the working environment in our institution. Of course, I could not tell him what exactly I felt like. I could only tell him that our institution could not afford high profile candidates like him and that they were looking for people suitable more for entry-level positions. I felt like being laughed at loudly!
Two or three years down the line, whenever I recall this incident or narrate it to someone, it never fails to bring a smile or two onto my face!

Jeyamathi. J

Ms. Jeyamathi, is a budding, innovative writer. She loves English a lot. She has successfully completed her Undergraduate degree on English Literature. Her love on English overflows as poems and short stories. Few of her writings can be seen in Instagram @verse_writer_maya.

PERSEVERANCE

The pearl inside the Shell,

Is perseverance.

The worm's transformation to silk,

Is perseverance.

The seed to plant,

Is perseverance.

The yolk to chick,

Is perseverance.

The little drops of rain from water vapor,

Is perseverance.

The revolution of earth,

Is perseverance.

The grass into paddy,

Is perseverance.

Lord Almighty soothed

All creatures with perseverance.

But – the miserable man

Is lacking in it.

Oh Lord! Please help,

These miserable creatures.

RESHMA

Reshma is a free verse writer. Her works expresses the valley of emotions. Her major works Explicates the truth about the existence and human compassion. According to her life is a mixed emotions which lets you to face bitter truths and also the beauty side of happiness.

SHADES OF LIFE

Beauties are not real.!

Heart is never faith the truth.!

Living is not a big thing.!

Character is never apart from others...!

Achieving success may come later.!

Believing other Will hurt sometimes!

Guiding with experience!

Everything Will come on time! Responsible for your position!

Everything will appear!

Only When spread love with others.

AJAY JAMES

Ajay James is a postgraduate in English and a novice writer. He strongly believes in the transformative powers of art. His self-proclaimed interests are reading and traveling, and he occasionally dabbles in cooking.

DARK

I looked into the abyss
Reflected in your eyes:
An unbreakable chain binds us
To a destiny of change
And a legacy of chaos.

I lost my mother to your will:
Her life snuffed out
By your calloused hands;
I watched, helpless and trapped,
As the light left her eyes.

The darkness of your soul, then
Falls on the love of my life:
I see her strength wane
And her spirit fails;
I see her death and I weep.
The past, the future,
Everything is connected;
Time makes fools of us all.
You are my worst nightmare—
I am you.

SURYA

Surya A is a Pre-service teacher. She is a portraitist and a naturalist. She habitually doodles, scribbles and loads her thoughts in an IG handle loaded thoughts. She is from the Southern tip of India, Kanyakumari.

OPEN THE DOOR

On a vicious lane,
the penniless children walk.
Holding the scars and pain,
deal with the void rock.
Striving to satiate the hunger,
survive as a lost singer.

The battered soul with sunken eyes,
Hollow cheeks having burnt palms,
Scrabby bairn wearing the exhausted duds,
bleeds throughout the childhood,
For a bowl of food and livelihood.

The melancholic wind,
and the teary wider sky,
empathize for the children.
None of us are blind.
Why don't we cry?
For the concealed children...
mere passive passers-by.
Why do we die?
All the day and night
in the rock of no light,
profoundly being voiceless
and perish being penurious.
Witnessing the sunset,
foreseeing the sunrise.

Mehansha E

Mehansha is a pre-service teacher based in Cape Camorin, Kanyakumari. She is an ardent lover of art and literature with a passion of writing poems as a medium of self-expression. She is a budding artist and writer and post her works in the IG handle @art.and.meh and @memoirs.of.meh

INTO THE WOODS

Into the woods I found myself

The ground was cold the trees were old

The breeze was heavy the river flow was wavy

The silence of the night made me fright

Saw the shimmering light of gold

Followed it with the heart of bold

Suddenly the light scattered

And lit the place with glitters

Amidst the sparkle I am

With the newly gotten wings

Hearing the angelic voice that sings

Followed it with eagerness

Roaming alone in the wilderness

When I heard his shuddering steps

My heart skipped a beat

Hid myself behind a tree

With an awaiting heart to foresee

Oh…No…what happened next?

I woke up from my dream

Mumbling the words "Who is he?"

Ishima Kayal Merimus. J. S

Celena is a 19-year-old novelist, with a burning passion to be on the screens someday. She gets most of the plotlines for her stories from her lucid dreams, or from her own experiences. Most of her works are grim, depressing and emotional, often aimed at pulling at the heartstrings of her readers, but they also end on a note of hope mostly, thus showing the readers that there's always light in the darkness of one's life

IN ANOTHER LIFE

Nothing new. The same old foggy windows, the same faulty heater, the same chill December winds making my hair stand on its end. I've forgotten how long I've been in this room, but I know that it's been too long that I've stopped counting the days.

"She could be depressed" I heard them say like six or seven months ago, give or take. According to my psychologist, I'm in a mindset where I'd take "Rash" decisions if I go out. So they decided to lock me in, not letting me get any form of human contact. It's not like I don't like this, but a girl can wish you know? How would it be to walk on the snowy sidewalk right now? Or on the icy blue lake frozen over *her* body..

Was it in March? I wouldn't know because time has come to standstill after that. Only the seasons that change now and then, tell me that it's been months. I somehow manage to find a picture from my messy drawer. It was of me and her on the day we

graduated school, with wide smiles on our faces. *It was as if*

everything, was just perfect.

In the picture, we were wearing our lucky charm bracelet, which I
still wear every single day, and has become the only thing
connecting me to

her. But I wonder if she was wearing it as she pushed herself down

into the deep waters?

Maybe I should get out there, to the lake. My parents, they would

never notice. They've probably forgotten that I even exist, because

they're more focused on my brother who has it all. A perfect GPA, a

sports scholarship, a pretty girlfriend, and in all, a nice life to look

forward to. If I had a perfect son like that, I'd forget about my

depressed daughter too.

After pocketing some of the stuff from my memory box, I manage to
open the stuck window. I peer out, and my eyes take in the first
glimpse of the world after a long while. The scent of Christmas
trees, the footsteps of people hurrying to

prepare for christmas eve, and the white snow glistening like a million tiny diamonds, remind me of that one Christmas that I got to spend over at her house.

I step out of the window, and carefully climb down the Persimmon tree growing in our neighbor's yard. I remember how easily she'd climb up this tree whenever I was confined to my room. I take off my shoes and set my feet on the snow, which may seem like something only a psycho would do; but at this point, I've stopped caring. The snow biting my feet actually felt good. But I know that I'll have to wear the shoe back on, if I were to make it to the lake without having frozen feet halfway. I walk quite slowly, taking my time to observe everything around me, while the sound of the snow crunching below my feet brings back a false sense of euphoria. And the people around me, they're all too busy to even notice a girl in just a shirt and sweatpants in the biting cold. It is as if no one wants to acknowledge my existence. My feet take me along the path I need to walk, very fluidly; the houses all look the same, has nothing really

changed in like eight months?

As I pass by an old playground, I'm filled with all the memories of

me and her, as kids, playing there all day long, with no worries of

the future, just giggling all the while. I smile to myself at the

thoughts, but the happiness lasts only for a second, before reality

sets in and sadness washes over.

I finally stand in front of the frozen lake, the eerie calmness of the place finally settling my unsettled mind. My nostrils are already closing up, but I'm not letting anything stop me today from walking on the frozen waters. The ice slightly cracks in places as I walk on it, the noise created piercing the silence of the lake. Would the ice give way? Probably. Do I care though? Not much. What do I have to lose? The smooth surface cracks for every step I take. Treading carefully, I come to the part of the lake right under a curvy overlooking cliff. *This was where she... jumped from.*

As I peer through the ice, I am overwhelmed with the millions of

emotions brimming up inside of me. I can still see her red hair

floating in the waters under my feet.

She didn't seem to have intentions to end her life this way, and no

one ever found her. But they said that they saw her jump off the

cliff. Why didn't they try to save her? Did they think that she was better off this way? How did your humanity fail when it came to saving her? I've asked all these questions a million times over and over in my head every single day that I spent locked up, but I've never gotten the answer. She was nobody's friend, but she was mine; she was all that I had; and she was the last thread that held my sanity together. Couldn't someone have jumped into the lake to pull her out? FOR MY SAKE AT LEAST?

I sound so selfish right now, ready to have her struggle with the demons in her mind, just so that I could stay sane. I've tried drowning myself in a bathtub, just to feel how she felt as the waters drowned her. It was a horrible feeling and I still can't comprehend why she had chosen this way to go.

She was always there for me; holding me up as I broke down, but I wasn't. I wasn't there when she ended herself. Maybe if I.. maybe if I had been there that day, maybe if I had, she'd have come to me and talked about it, rather than trying to stop her breath?

But now that it has happened, maybe someday this ice would melt apart and reveal her? Maybe they'd find her floating around, finally having attained the sense of peace she was after?

Maybe. Isn't life just a game of maybes?

I stare at my reflection, but the frozen blue of the lake stares back at me, like her piercing blue eyes did before. My palms imprint themselves on the ice, leaving a mark saying I was here. I wonder what she did when her life pulled itself out. Did she call my name as the waters pulled her down forever? Did she struggle towards the end or bid farewell with a smile?

I put my right ear to the ice, with a desperate hope to hear her once more.. But I only hear the sound of the layers of ice slightly cracking, the sound of the wind howling, and along with that, the sound of my own heart, thumping inside its cage.

My hands are numb, my hair is piled with snow, and my eyes are closing slowly, trying to save themselves from the harsh chill. I take out the things I put inside my pockets. After a long look at the graduation photo of me and her one last time, I light it up with a lighter. A small warmth spreads through the cold as it burns down to ashes; but there isn't still enough warmth to warm up my icy cold self.

I feel her presence lingering nearby, probably telling me to go home, telling me to save myself from the biting cold. jasmine Why don't I come after you? Why don't I let this cold freeze my body over? The snow's already threatening to stop my veins from pumping blood. Why don't I let my body lay here for an hour more, watching you through this frozen glass? Why do I have to let you go when I could follow you?

But I know that you would never want that for me; you would never let me come after you. But still I lay here, freezing in the snow,to bid a last farewell to your frozen self, six feet under a frozen lake. Maybe I'll let you go in this life, hoping that you'd come back to me in another.

"Goodbye my love, until we meet again, in another life."

ROSHINI M J

Roshini MJ loves to write poetry about her saviour, Jesus Christ. All her writings center around faith and positivity. She is a research scholar too. Soli Deo Gloria!

THE TREE AND THE FRUIT

In the garden of goodness he placed me.

I wandered here and there,

Not knowing where to go.

But His kindness chased me,

And gave me a chance with a warning-

To change my mourning into dancing,

For He was ever - loving!

Even though I was running away from Him

He kept tuning my ways towards Him.

He spoke with a spark to cleanse my scars:

"The axe is near the root of the tree,

May your bear good fruit to be free."

He gave me the best support system- His words!

As I repent - He was waiting there,

To make me blossom through His blessings.

Yes! He warns and cares:

He is JESUS CHRIST, My Saviour.

He decides all the shades of my life-My Maker.

Shoumiya Preethy Prabakar

Shoumiya Preethy Prabakar is a final year student in a dental college in Tamil Nādu, India. She's a passionate writer with themes of her own. She's simple with her words and also writes beautiful quotes. She got her interest in writing when she happened to randomly spoke a line ' Fireflies are meant to light up the darkness that has bestowed our hearts '. She also manages a blog on word press https://revivingthethoughts.wordpress.com/blog-2/

TRIBUTE TO PARENTS

What better would you look up to when you have your parents out there, pulling out their legs to give you all that you need and when they are there sacrificing all of theirs to enlighten you. Miles away maybe your parents now, working just to ensure the family is built with perfect basement and developed with all that's required to finish its construction.

What our eyes see to things that fantasize is just the richness and not their handwork and the years of effort they've done. Well yes infact it's not your fault to think that way. You have your freedom to speech and thoughts and endless may the list be. It's the views of the people who know you in distance. But I could maybe bring some change in opinion.

We might have not seen our parents work, or maybe some of us are not even aware of what their work is. Allow me to shake up your heads, to remind you we must know them. They play their roles and indeed we must play ours. Some of us might say they don't understand me, but ping yourself, have you understood them once in a million pointless fights you've had till date. If yes, stay blessed. If not , worry less and start understanding the ones who brought you to this world.

Nevertheless it would be the least thing every parent would expect from their beloved children to 'understand' them. I don't speak of evil parents thou, I hope you getting whom I refer about because they're not considered in the list.

Understanding doesn't need so much hard work, it just needs all of your heart and minds in it. Okei, I'm not listing out advices or anything, I just wanted to convey and ask you to act as a responsible child and make an effort to peek through their minds.

All that they did before bringing you into this universe is totally different from what they're now. And so should be our responsibilities from infants to adulthood, may what the age be but just a matter of fact you'll still be their child. Adding up to this, that they'll still work for you even after giving you in hands in marriage as grand-parents and great-grand-parents.

Their life is like run and run till you beat up the bush to fire and roar and that's how it would be when you become a parent.

Parents, are like the ones with so much of clogged experiences and frozen feelings with an overflow of work brimmed to their cup. Their peace of mind comes only in a sound sleep with calm mind after a good meal. And of course, to be noted; their children, they become the most sensitive when they have to leave their parents and go for higher studies. It's like so much of agitated sentiments stuck to four corners of the room and just not able to express their expressions thinking not to create a sentimental scenario out there because they're parents have nourished them with boldness in their upbringing. And well yes, so do they with a masked up face and beautiful smiles displayed. We fear the most with minds filled to act with all due respect to their upbringing. They stay out and they work for us so that we have all the happiness we could have. That is where they sacrifice theirs. Working with, fear of the fact to be fired from workplace due to confidential reasons. And what less.

You may be in a joint family or maybe a nuclear one or maybe away from them or as a payguest but you would never find better people than your parents. Some of us are dear darling children and shower all our love when we're next to them and few are just not expressive but have ofcourse got gentle feelings within and a few seems inhuman to people with nothing but buried emotions and love.

I can assure you no better and best would anyone lookafter you than your parents. They're the heaven-given gifts to us. Philosophically they're the Image of the Almighty you worship.

Honour them with your achievements and give them the priceless pride they deserve.

HIMADRI SHEKHAR DUTTA

Himadri Shekhar Dutta is presently working as Assistant Professor of English at St. Xavier's College, Dumka which is also his hometown. He is an academic writer and poet in weekends. His other interests are in crime and spy genres.

UMBRELLA

I still remember those showers

When you forgot your umbrella

And came drenched

Water dripping from your shrug as nectar.

Oh! How I longed

I longed

That you do not catch a cold

Yet shower me bliss every rainy day

And that is why

I could never gift you an umbrella

Ambita C J

Ambita C J is an M.A graduate in English Literature born in Neyyoor of Kanyakumari District, currently doing her B.Ed. degree. She has great love for music, art, literature and photography. Pursuing knowledge about ample things and exploring the unknown things as her goal, she is a passionate writer. "His Masterpiece" is her first poem in which she has dedicated to God. The poem tells her emotional feelings and thoughts of finding God.

HIS MASTERPIECE

They told me in my childhood that He is in the skies,

When I looked above, I felt as I was looking something greater than all;

They told me in my teenage that He is in my heart,

When I searched my heart, I felt that is not possible because He was pure;

They told me in my youth that He is everywhere,

When I saw everywhere, I felt that something great is present around me;

As I get older

I find Him everywhere

In the skies

In the trees

In the ocean

In the hills

I feel Him in everywhere of His creativity;

Now I feel Him in my heart,

He is everywhere and anywhere,

I am also His Masterpiece of His creativity.

Zaffar Iqbal

Zaffar Iqbal is a young writer and growing critic in English literature. He is hailing from Jammu and Kashmir India. He studied from Jammu University state university and then Central University Of Punjab Bathinda India. He is a college topper, he is adjoined different social activists organization like NSYF etc. He is an ex Captain of Students' Union at college days. He always wants to became a writer. In his college days he studied The scarlet letter and The rape of lock and and Who's afraid of Virginia Woolf by Nathaniel Hawthorne, Alexander Pope and by Edward Albee respectively and more of Literature. He by himself wrote some articles as "My Innocent Society" mara becahra samaaj , and a poem " My mistress is very clever by heart " and a famous short story "The Hate" in which he used characters of Roger and Anar Kali..

TO WHOM I LOVE

I love to enjoy the evening's scene . It's natural glimpse , I love to enjoy nature , because no man can discover anything to compare with the Allah's creations.

Whenever I feels myself alone , I love to go to there (a space where I can easily target the glimpse.

I want to go in the depth of nature and it's factual background.

I love to have a look on glimpse of the shining star at night 9'o clock.

Whenever I feels myself alone I usually started to go on the out corner of my house, I want to fully romance with the natural flowers, which are looking and shining like stars on the tree at the front of my house.

I usually want to click the evening's pictures and the of different flowers and somehow branches of trees . I love the sparrows and their kids living in the front side of my balcony and made a nest their.I love to go outside of covered area like home , while it's raining outside. I want to enjoy the beauty of rain , as In our Kashmir usually it's happens even at 12'o PM clock a day.

I love to talk to the old people and to share their loneliness. I love to children and their smile and as when they copy mine smile.

SILPA SRIKUMAR

Silpa Srikumar grew up in Alappuzha, Kerala. She's a teacher and when she's not surrounding herself with words you can find her doing painting.

EMBED

These four walls are shrinking;
 I can no longer see my own shadow,
The colors I've seen in your eyes are fading.
Allow me to float in your eyes with your colors.

Every morning, I shed my leaves because I had lost my home.
Be my tree, a place where I can be cherished for who I am.
Be my strong root, on which I can stand
when the howling gales blow.

These four walls are shrinking,
where I can no longer water myself.
Where I am unable to fertilize my land,
the seed within me seeks to grow.
The land in me is parched and longing for rain.

ANNE BENITA

Anne Benita D is a budding author who loves to write on the themes of true lives. Her first book entitled "The Hidden Reality of Life" also went through such interesting titles. She is also a co-author in many works. Her interest grows much more in writing to bring out more writings.

ONE ACCORD

Strings lined up in one accord,
Carried the music for the world;
Reasons brawled within that accord,
Brawls became the joy of the world;
Marched on, marched on, in one accord,
Searched the wings of the world.

Time changed, season changed,
In one accord, strings stood;
Man changed, humanity changed,
In the air, music stood;
Felt suppressed in life, the heart changed,
Searching for the wings from where he stood.

Light shone far away from his shore,
Love went far away from his heart;
Tribulations blew in his path from the other shore,
Excruciating pain hurried into his heart;
Waiting for better things in the corridor from that shore,
Buried the weakness to stand steady from his heart.

Jessima Begum

Jessima Begum, poetess and writer from Tamil Nadu write under the pen name of Jade Begy. She completed her bachelor's degree. Highly influenced by the folklores by her grandmother and great works of English Literature, she has a passion for writing. In her works, one can find the blend of folk culture with modernity.

THE SURVIVAL

In a village, there lived a young girl named Meeka who's the fourth daughter of Hailey and Kennan, a farmer couple with 7 children. Kennan a lazy, nothing-to-do, selfish farmer ill-treats his wife and beats his children. Hailey, the breadwinner of the family, does some labour works and also farming the yields and loves her children the most as she tolerates the torture of her spouse.

Kennan, as a worthless father, arranged marriages to her daughters at a very young age to the old men like sold cattle in a market. Therefore, Subbie, Any and Fira, the elder daughters of Meeka were married at the age of 15 to the local guards who were of twice older than them.

Meeka, 10 years old girl, who wants to support her family financially like her mother, Hailey through educate herself and her younger brother, Allen and younger sisters, Dolly and Rehaam. But, at the age of 15, she too has face the same situation like her elder sisters. Kennan forced Meeka to marry a travel agent; Fortunately, Meeka was saved by Hailey and School teacher, Mona. In an anger, Kennan stopped her studies and Meeka forced to do household works. With the help of Allen, Meeka was able to read and write.

Years went on; At the age of 21, Meeka was married to clerk named Joah and after one year of marriage, Meeka was blessed with a girl child, Jade. Her marriage life was not a happy one; Joah, a careless man who did not spent much time with Meeka; he often goes to city for an official visit and leaving Meeka and his child alone in the village. Meeka felt loneliness and wanted to get Joah's love and attention to her. In order to escape from the loneliness, she used to write letters to his mother and siblings and played with her 1-year-old baby girl, Jade.

In order to gain his attention, Meeka decide to go with him when he has a visit to city. Her dream has come true one day, Meeka and Joah prepared their packings to move to city. They planned a 1 week trip to the city and Meeka was so excited to see the city. The family reached the city at night and Joah booked a room for stay at the hotel named Ruby which made Meeka to remember the incident in her childhood when her teacher, Mona showed a jewel made up of ruby stones for her marriage.

The next day, Joah took Meeka and his child, Jade to travel around the city. He took them to park, mall, theatre, etc., to enjoy their trip. Meeka was fascinated by the colours of the city. They returned to the hotel at evening and Meeka narrated her first day experience in the city through a letter to his mother and slept well with a joy.

The second day, the city seemed too pretty as it has a carnival. Everywhere in the city, people were crowded. Joah took Meeka and Jade to the carnival and planned to enjoy the rides in it. He left Meeka and Jade in a toy shop and went to have a ride in a Giant-wheel. Meanwhile, Meeka was too busy to select a toy for her child and not even noticed her husband left them. After realising that she was lost, Meeka was frightened by the crowd in the carnival. She was almost fainted to cry with her child in her hand and searched Joah in the carnival. Joah, on the other hand, enjoyed the ride in Giant-wheel and completely forgot about Meeka and returned to the hotel and slept.

Meeka sobbed bitterly and wanted to go to hotel whether she was able to find Joah at there. But, she did not know the way to return to the hotel except the name of the hotel, Ruby. On her struggle to find a way, Meeka first encountered a Prostitute who forced her to do her profession. She lost the hope to live. Meeka was saved from the prostitute by a writer and took her to a nearby coffee shop and asked about her. Meeka told everything about her. The writer was also new to the city; so he did not know about the hotel. Fortunately, the attending waiter for their table knew the phone number of the hotel, Ruby while hearing to their conversation.

After a good peaceful sleep, Joah woke up and realised that Meeka and his child were not there. He went to the reception where he received the call of a writer about Meeka and his child, he rushed to the coffee shop. On seeing Joah, Meeka had a hope to live, yet Joah scolded her like anything. The writer and the waiter felt pity for Meeka and her child to have a relation like Joah. Meeka insisted Joah to leave the city right now and they reached the village at late night.

J. M. ROJITH RAJA

His name is Rojith Raja. A personal experience have driven him to write poems. Currently, He is doing BA English at Hindustan College.

THE LOVE JUICE

An Enchanter dropped a love juice in my eyes

When I were asleep,

For, the juice contained the beauty of first glance

So that I could fall in love with my beloved,

My sweetheart arrived from the paradise

For, All the earthly beings bowed her,

The entire place was filled with holiness

So that no sinners could stand there,

Birds sung, Beasts rejoiced, Dolphins jumped through the hoops.

All creatures were happy.

Nevertheless, there was no sign of love from her

She merely looked at me,

I were broken, weakened and saddened.

I had to live with her memory

There was no other choice,

Greif had swallowed me,

Darkness had surrounded me,

Agony had destroyed me,

Happiness had left me,

Even devil was exhausted for bringing pain,

But, I knew my suffering was vain,

It just happened for my gain,

GREESHMA RP

She is an emerging admirer of poetry. Her interest in learning new words paved way to writing. She follows a typical story in poetry.

BEING LOCKED

DAYS AND DATES

Where it all started,

When it all stayed,

There it all resides;

Here it all revives;

Deep in my Heart ♡ ♡

MOMENTS AND MEMORIES

Why it's a memory!

A memory to resound

How it's a moment

A Moment to reckon.

Deep in my thoughts………………..

LOVE AND LIFE

Then a moment to start the love,

On a day towards unconditional

Here a memory to stay in life

With a date towards unknown

Depth of my Soul ♡ ♡ ♡

Ramsha Zaheen

Ramsha Zaheen is second year student of IGNO, Lucknow , currently pursuing M.A in english. She has started writing poems at an early age. Few of her poems has been published in the past days. Currently based in Lucknow she wishes to go to the places which have captivating and mesmerizing natural beauty. Being very close to the nature she finds peace in it. She is fond of painting, reading and writing poetry.

THE TEMPTING LIES

Lies, served in golden ivorian platter of words
Embellished with silvery expectations
Are often tempting
Shrouding the dark reality
Beneath the velvety deceptions

Tearing the trust apart
Breaking the innocent heart
Turning dreams to dust
Leaving the rest to rust

You know why these lies are tempting
Because they take us far from ugly truths
As a human we cling to them
Grabbing the noxious yet toothsome morsel

World is full of tempting lies
Beautiful as the feathers of butterfly
Die as soon as someone catches it
Not to live a wholesome life

Book Benchers

Lies are what?

Captivating landscapes in the filthy world

Or a castle in the mid with hollow walls

Filled with void and numbness and all

Or a mirage to quench the thirst

Of the one who

Escaped from dungeons of dark truths

Overburdened with ugly truths

Mortals find solace in tempting lies

But, Truth how brutal and harsh

Never fills the mind and heart

With guilt and remorse

Without spilling the beans of course.

Smita

Smita is a teacher by profession and she has a flair for writing poetry and short stories. She is a fun-loving person who lives in each moment and enjoys it.

Shades of Life

SET ME FREE......

What mistake did I make?

To deserve this venomous bait....

I know my words set fire....

But what less do I desire....

This world has shaken the human in me,

 The joker in me is on the spree,

 Beware you venomous snakes,

Don't spill poison in my 'stake'...

The judgments, vengeance are all going to vanish,

The words and memories leave you to banish...

Your acts remain before and after your life,

You can choose to make them sourly rife....

Before you think what puzzle is this verse,

Read again and know that you won't diverse,

It's the story of an emotional fool,

Who is ready to be pushed in the pool,

But it's voluntarily done to abide the rule of life and love....

And cry benign "et tu brute"....

A voice echoes in the woods far away,

"Why did you ditch yourself for them?"

I answered bleakly with strain...

"Just for setting myself free from this pain..."

ADHITHYA

She, a lady with eternal love for words, who proposes it often for its unleashing elegance not minding even if it rejects her. She's passionate post graduate literature student who takes up writing as a painkiller that pours in the spirit of positivity! She loves editing videos and has a great love in putting poems as videos. Thus she does much of it. Look at her works with her id @word_O_licious

THE WEEPER IN SOLITUDE

Pacifying each other

In front of a coffin,

For someone is

Lying still amongst

The calm mob around

With disheartening notion,

In the agony of grief!

Floating memories

Fleeted dreams

Frowning anxiety

Foul aromas

Failure of hope

Freaky family

After hours of woe

Penetrating all souls,

There came an end

A four legged giant

Had come to bear that

Ever Hibernating being...

The corpse was buried

Forfeiting to Nature

The crowd dispersed

Wanting him back

Shedding river of tears

With the falling rains

Someone is still

Found with snivel

With a dishevel,

As her hope in vein,

Forcefully she turned back

With his ticket to heaven!

YAMUNA SRUTHI DEV

This is Sruthi. She has developed a love for books ever since she was 9 and has won numerous prizes for writing and oration. She spends most of her free time reading. Her favourite authors include Ruskin Bond, O' Henry, Roald Dahl & Jane Austen among many others. She finds reading to be an escape from all that is fast happening in the world. It fills her with joy whenever she come across a great literary work and is left in awe of it for quite some time. Literature is a vast ocean of talent and to say that she is part of even a tiny ounce of it makes her so proud. Here she has written a poem, something she came up with rather quickly, but made her feel really good about the way she wrote it. Hope you like it as much as she does.

HOAX SHINE

I've an inkling about clouds,

they lash down every time they feel heavy,

and we feel impish glee of their agony.

It's not like they don't try to hold it,

but it finds peace where the droplets and the land meet.

The drops of the rain don't have a voice,

we hear thunder

it's that heart making a weeping noise,

we are so malevolent with our thoughts of their function,

we rejoice ever time rain splatters,

and when it slows down, we are all flattered.

When the sunlight and the rain rendezvous,

we find charm in that striking chaos.

We tell ourselves that, that hoax shine is alright

and that it'll be the same, the whole time.

It's hurting because

we think the same way for mankind.

Nasria MS

Nasria MS is currently working as Assistant Professor of English in Kodaikanal Christian College. She has done her Post Graduation in English Literature from the English and Foreign Languages University, Hyderabad. She loves black coffee and writing poetry.

AN ORDINARY HERO

My grandpa, a man of 70

 Monday to Saturday rides his cycle

To work at a textile store

Never have I seen him otherwise.

An ordinary teacher of healthy living

 Amidst multitudes of those monstrosities

Those sickly dragons breathing fumes of grey.

 And yet nobody applauded my grandpa

 Nobody hailed him for his simplicity

Nobody revered him for his choice of the cycle

I believe admiration surges in our hypocritical hearts

 Only for the make-believe Achillean heroes

Those heroes towering and flying against injustice

And grooving with slender women

On the silver screen.

Unfortunately my grandpa, a man of 70

 Riding his cycle from Monday to Saturday

Is a man exceptionally ordinary.

Shades of Life

SATHIYA SEELAN

I SATHIYASEELAN Assistant Professor AVC College
Autonomous Mannampandal Mayiladuthurai Tamil Nadu

CORONA- THE DEVIL

The devil captures your breath, plunder your time.

The devil grabs the bright light of life.

Life is barren, souls are restless,

Roads are vacant, people are careless.

Happens in movies, all came real,

With fear in our hearts, confront to challenge!

You think you arrested us, oh devil!

We feel protected, secure in our homes.

Battle to win back our mind,

Brawl to what we must still find.

If you must go out guess twice,

Always wear a mask, be careful!

After arrival home, sanitise,

Or wash your hands at least twice.

Covid-19 is the name,

It is playing a violent game.

Alert your strength,

For health is our treasure!

Finally, there are no tears to come crawling in,

Relative, we found a way to accept it!

GOLDLIN PEARLY J.

GOLDLIN PEARLY J A, author of the poem LEARNED TO BE WHAT! completed her masters in English literature and currently doing her research in Indian Writing in English. She loves Nature and interested in Cultural studies, Eco-criticism and Feminism.

LEARNED TO BE WHAT!

Learned to be what?

Courageous or cautious,

Introvert or extrovert,

Modern or tradition…

Loving or hating,

Beauty or ugly,

Feasible or permissible…

Learn to be what?

Learn to love what you like

Learn to make what you want

Learn to be happy

Learn to make others happy

Learn not to expect others love

Learn to spread love

Learn to showcase your inner beauty peace and love

Learn to appreciate others

Learn to not discourage anyone

Learn to love your parents

Learn not to dwell them in orphanage

 Learn to love – and

Learn to be loved.

ANALIN SHAJEN

Analin Shajen A is one who scribbles words and then arranges those in such a way so that the one who reads it will understand what he expects. He is a nestling who has just spread his wings in the blue sky of literature. Usually there will be a deep meaning and emotion in his writings.

WITH THE MOON

And it's nothing but a moon

I met in the month next to June

It came close not very soon

Then there was a beautiful monsoon

The moon and I shared a tiny cocoon

But here and there faced terrible typhoon

Wished to give her heaven as a boon

But pushed her in hell what a misfortune!

In deep guilt I m losing my immune

Which pushes me to the state of goon

May be the medicine is her laughing tune

No need of much but just a table spoon

Now certain things burst like balloon

We still wait for the end of the doom

The moon and I will be inviting you for a noon.

Tanvi Punia

Tanvi Punia is a 21-year-old blogger and content writer from Haryana. She pursued a Bachelor's Degree in English Honours from Kurukshetra University, Kurukshetra. For years, she has had a passion for writing, so she decided to own that role and be intentional about it. She has worked for various companies and start-ups around the world as a content writer. Currently, she is the Content Head at an e-commerce platform named TrueGether. She enjoys reading books, listening to podcasts, playing chess, and watching content over the OTT platforms.

LIVE LIFE TO THE FULLEST: BE THE BEST VERSIONS OF YOURSELVES!

We are living in extremely hectic times. In reality, time appears to be our most valuable asset, as well as the most difficult to manage. Not just because there are endless events, projects, sports to participate in, things to learn, places to see, and different sorts of art to admire, but also because diversions abound and the entertainment world "steals" our time.

People perceive happiness in a variety of ways and hold a variety of attitudes about it, depending on the culture in which they live. I've listed down four strategies to boost your happiness in everyday life and answer the question, "How can I live a happy life?"

- *Meditate, Be Grateful, and Put Your Positive Thoughts to Play*

These are some excellent methods for cultivating a positive attitude. According to various studies, these techniques, when combined with the development of healthy thinking patterns, can help minimize sadness, anxiety, and emotional weariness at work, as well as strengthen a person's immune system.

- *Build Lasting Relationships*

Aside from meditation, begin to think more about the well-being of others and less about yourselves and your worldly needs. In fact, minds that are designed for compassion and kindness are more likely to experience sentiments of happiness.

- *Healthy Bodies, Happy Minds*

Physical health has an impact on psychological well-being. Regular walks and a balanced diet have been linked to increased levels of creativity and energy during the day. Furthermore, spending more time in nature is linked to increased sentiments of happiness.

- *Give Importance to Well Being*

Accepting that life isn't supposed to be filled with exclusively good times is crucial. We should strive for something other than happiness: Well-Being. Life will never be all about having a good time, full of smiles, and providing you with an easy and delightful experience. Develop your emotional intelligence and see life as a place where you can go through all of these feelings.

Nighil S Toms

Nighil S Toms, is from Kerala, God's own country. After his studies from India and Australia, he started his career as an educationalist by starting Goan Institute International Consociation of Education Pvt .Ltd. in 2007, a skill development company trained many school and college students across India more than a decade. Later he started Jeevdhaan Health Care Pvt. Ltd.,a GMP Certified Ayurvedic and Cosmetic manufacturing Company in 2015.A life long story teller and poet, Nighil Toms specializes in narrating life experiences packed with dreams and romance. When he is not writing, he spends most of his time in reading and in the administration affairs of his companies

THE UNSAID STORIES

I want to tell you my stories- the 'unsaid stories'

The treasures which I kept for a life time …

Till the polar star fade under the morning sky

Let the night birds watch us once they get up

And the moon listen the rhythm of your heart beats

The powerful song and the music which could give

Strength and life even to a dying man!

Let's stay up till the dawn and share the unsaid stories

And speak about them- 'the shadows of the world'!

They say life is what we make it and life is crystal

Like a rain drop of the first rain after the summer

They are right- let's keep it close to our hearts.

If the rain drop battered and bruised

Shattered or drained by the time or the fate …

Smile at life and continue the walk   with a new spirit.

Walk to the other end and feel the crisp sea breeze

And stay under the shade trees till the turn of tides

Let the breeze sing with the waves the 'unsung ragas'

To cherish the memories of a life time…

They say love is noisy   like a roaring wave, it shouts

Always for the silent, dreamy and crushed sand!

Never trust them blindly-it's an imposture!

Butterflies teach us how they love a flower silently.

They say they will hold your hands when you are

In a strange land, once you lose the way in your life

Never believe it blindly –it's an imposture!

They will leave you alone and turn the face

Believe in your shadows not of the shade trees

Search for a mirror, even a broken piece

To see the real reflection of ' you -the winner'

Broken things reflect the real life and the

Broken souls get greater power after each fall

Oh! It's about to see the dawn, we are late…

Let's stand on our own and find our ways

And figure out the ways for a horse sacrifice

To conquer the conquest of life till the last breath

And wish the world a happy day with a

Smile from the heart to the hearts

Shades of Life

Mrs. Benila

Mrs. Benila is a multi-talented, budding writer and erudite Scholar who loves to express her agony through writing. Aspiring to be a teacher, she is pursuing her Doctoral studies and is widely interested in Feminism."

LIFE

Life...

Is a chance

With a number of shades.

One life to live

Which can never be retrieved.

Be thankful

To God for every shade of life.

Every new day

Brings plenty of experiences

And loads of memories.

Your life can only

Be loved and lived by you.

Every day is a gift

That adds new

Colour to lead

A happy life.

Book Benchers